Addison Wesley

3

Science&
Technology

Addison Wesley
Science & Technology 3

Earth and Space Systems

Soil

Ricki Wortzman
Grade 3 Program Authors:

Nora L. Alexander   Carole Moult
Doug Herridge   Ricki Wortzman

Addison Wesley

Toronto

Coordinating & Developmental Editors
Jenny Armstrong
Lynne Gulliver

Editors   **Researcher**
Debbie Davies   Siobhan Dooley, Pronk&Associates
Jackie Dulson
Christy Hayhoe

Reviewers
Alice Castleman, Association for Canadian Educational Resources
Sandra Fazio, John T. Tuck Elementary, Halton District School Board
Katherine Shaw, Miller's Grove School, Peel Board of Education

Pearson Education Canada would like to thank the teachers and consultants
who reviewed and field-tested this material.

Design
Pronk&Associates

ISBN 0–201–64979–9

This book contains recycled product and is acid free.
Printed and bound in Canada.

2 3 4 5 – TCP – 04 03 02 01 00

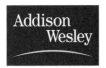

Soil

Soil is everywhere! No matter where you go, you will always find soil. The soil you see in different places can look, feel, and even smell different. Living things all around the world need soil to survive.

Now you will find out:

- how soil is made
- what happens when water moves through or on soil
- why people, animals, and plants need soil
- how soil is used to make things

Soil Is Important

You walk and play on soil. Maybe you don't think about it very much. But when you do, you realize that humans can't live without soil. Most living things depend on soil in some way. Can you think of reasons why?

Work On It

1. Look at the picture with a partner. How is soil important?

2. Make a list of your ideas.

3. Can you think of any other ways soil is important? Add these to your list.

Communicate

1. Draw a picture of one way soil is important to you.

1

A Cupful of Soil

You have used soil in many different ways. Perhaps you have made a sand castle or a mud pie. But have you ever looked closely at soil? What do you think you can find in a cup of soil?

Work On It

What does soil look like? What does it feel like? Does it have a smell? Does it make a sound when you rub it between your fingers? Take a close look at a cup of soil and find out.

What You Need

- Newspaper
- A cup of soil
- A magnifying lens
- Toothpicks

What You Will Do

1 Cover your work space with newspaper. Spread out your soil sample.

2 Look closely at the soil.

3 Sort the soil. Use a toothpick to move the pieces into groups.

4 Draw a picture of the groups you made.

Safety Caution

If you are to collect a soil sample, your teacher will tell you safe places so that you don't harm plants or animals. Always wash your hands after handling soil.

Communicate

1. What did you find in the soil?

2. What did you find the most of in your soil sample?

Build On What You Know

Put the soil in a container and water it. Keep the soil moist. Watch to see if anything grows.

What Is Soil Made Of?

You have looked at soil very carefully. Now you will find out what soil is made of.

Moving water, wind, plants, and changes in temperature can crack large rocks. Over a very long time, large rocks are broken into tiny pieces. These tiny pieces of rocks and minerals are a part of soil.

Soil has spaces in it. These spaces are filled with water and air.

Dead animals and plants decay and break down into tiny pieces. These rotted plants and animals make a part of soil called **humus**. Humus is very dark brown. It crumbles when you touch it. Humus mixes with tiny rocks, air, and water to form soil.

Now you know that all soil has four non-living parts. Soil contains rocks, air, water, and humus.

Look at the pictures. Work with a partner. Say whether the soil in each picture has more rocks, air, water, or humus.

Communicate

1. What does soil contain?

2. What kind of soil do you think you would find in a garden plot?

3. What kind of soil do you think you would find in your schoolyard?

Build On What You Know

Did you find any other things when you looked at your cup of soil in **Activity 1: A Cupful of Soil?** Add them to your list from question 1.

3

Comparing Soil

There are many different kinds of rocks, plants, and animals on Earth. That means there must be many different kinds of soil. Soil can be different colours. Some soil is very dry. Soil might crumble when you squeeze it in your hand. Some soil is sticky and holds together.

Work On It

What makes one soil sample different from another? Take a close look at different types of soil. Find out how they are the same and how they are different.

What You Need

- Newspaper
- 3 different soil samples
- A magnifying lens
- Toothpicks

What You Will Do

1 **a.** Cover your work space with newspaper. Draw three large circles on the newspaper.

  b. Number each circle.

2 Put a different soil sample in each circle.

3 Observe the soil sample labelled 1. Use a magnifying lens and toothpicks to help you.

4 Use your sense of touch, smell, and sight to describe the sample. Record your findings in a chart like this one.

	Touch	Smell	Sight	Colour
1	grainy	no smell	no lumps	light brown
2				
3				

5 **a.** Use your senses to describe the samples in circles 2 and 3.

  b. Record your findings in the chart.

Safety Caution

Never put soil in your mouth. Remember to wash your hands after handling soil.

Communicate

1. a. In what ways were your soil samples the same?

  b. In what ways were they different?

2. a. Which type of soil do you think is good for growing things?

  b. Why do you think that?

Build On What You Know

What do you think is different about the soil in your playground, your backyard, and your local park? Gather soil from different areas and test it. Add the results to your chart.

4

Separating Soil

Get Started

The three main kinds of rock pieces in soil are sand, clay, and silt. Sand pieces are the largest; they feel gritty. Silt pieces are not as big as sand; they feel like powder. Clay pieces are the smallest; they feel smooth and are sticky when wet. Different types of soil can have different amounts of sand, silt, and clay.

Sandy soil is loose and does not hold water well. Most plants do not grow well in this soil.

Soil that has silt in it holds water well. But this kind of soil can be blown away by the wind.

Soil that has clay holds water very well. The grains are so small and tightly packed that plants do not grow well in it.

Loam is a mixture of sand, clay, and silt. Loam often contains humus and is useful to gardeners. It holds water and has the nutrients plants need.

Work On It

In this investigation, you will separate a soil sample. You will find out how much sand, silt, and clay is in the sample.

What You Need..

- A glass jar with a lid
- A soil sample
- A container of water

What You Will Do..

1 **a.** Fill your jar about one-third full with soil.

b. Add water until the jar is almost full.

2 Draw a picture of what the jar looks like.

3 Put the lid on the jar tightly. Shake the jar.

4 **a.** Wait five minutes, then draw what you see in your jar.

b. Label your picture with the date.

c. Put your jar in a place where it won't be disturbed.

5 **a.** The next day, draw what you see in your jar.

b. Label your picture with the date.

Communicate

1. Label the drawing of your jar to show which part is clay, which part is silt, and which part is sand.

2. Compare your sample with other groups' samples. What do you find?

How Much Water?

Get Started

All plants need water to grow. Some plants can grow with just a little water from the soil. Other plants need a lot of water. Plants also need air from the soil. Most plants will drown if there is too much water in the soil because the water fills the spaces where air should be.

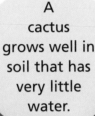

A cactus grows well in soil that has very little water.

This water hyacinth grows best in water. Can you think of other plants like this one?

Work On It

When water is added to soil, the soil holds some of the water. The rest of the water passes through the soil. You will plan an investigation to find out whether sand, clay, or loam holds the most water.

What You Need

- Equal amounts of sand, loam, clay
- A graduated cylinder of water

What You Will Do

Follow these steps to plan your investigation.

Step 1: Which soil sample do you think will hold the most water? Record your prediction.

Step 2: Draw a diagram to show how you will set up your investigation.

Step 3: What materials will you need? List them.

Step 4: Do your investigation. Record your results.

Step 5: Answer the question: Which soil sample holds the most water? Be ready to explain your answer.

You might want to use a chart like this one to record your results.

	Soil A	Soil B	Soil C
mL of water drained			

Communicate

1. What did you find out in this investigation?

2. Which soil sample let the most water drain through?

3. a. Which soil sample do you think is best for growing plants?

   b. Why did you choose that soil?

Build On What You Know

Look at the three soil samples after the water has been poured through them. What differences do you see?

6 Planting Seeds

This land has rich soil. This soil is good for growing many types of plants.

One reason why soil is important is because plants grow in it. You have observed that soil can be different. What do you think makes soil good for growing things?

In this investigation, you will compare how well seeds grow in different soils.

What You Need

- Water
- 3 small paper cups
- 3 types of soil: clay, sand, loam
- A measuring cup
- A pencil
- Radish seeds

What You Will Do

1 **a.** Fill each paper cup with the same amount of a different type of soil.

b. Label the cups to say if the soil is sand, clay, or loam.

2 Use a pencil to make a shallow hole in each cup of soil.

3 Drop three radish seeds in each hole and cover each hole with soil.

4 **a.** Add the same amount of water to each cup.

b. Put the cups in a warm, sunny place.

5 **a.** Observe your cups every day.

b. Add water to make sure the soil never dries out. Remember to add the same amount of water to each cup.

c. Record your observations.

Communicate

1. a. Which soil is better for growing radish seeds?

b. How do you know?

2. Why do you think this soil is better for growing things?

Build On What You Know

In **Activity 4: Separating Soil** you found out how much sand, silt, and clay were in soil samples. How do you think information like this might be helpful to farmers and gardeners?

7 Can You Compost?

Get Started

Soil with humus is good for growing many types of plants. Gardeners and farmers add humus to soil to make it better for growing things. Humus is made from decaying plant matter. This process is called composting.

Ingredients

- A large container
- Vegetable and fruit peelings
- Other organic waste like leaves, grass clippings, eggshells, tea leaves, and coffee grounds
- Water
- Soil
- A long stick for stirring

1 Take the container outside. Put soil in the bottom.

2 Add vegetable and fruit peelings and other waste.

3 Add water to make everything damp.

4 Put another layer of soil on top.

5 Repeat the layers.

6 Every week, stir well with the long stick.

7 After about two months, you will have humus! It is ready to add to your garden.

People make a lot of waste that can help the Earth.

1. Read the recipe for making humus.

2. Draw a picture of what you think a compost heap looks like.

3. Find the compost sites in this neighbourhood.

Communicate

1. **a.** Does your school have a compost container?

   b. Do you think it should? Tell why or why not.

2. Why do you think some people leave grass clippings on the lawn after they cut the grass?

3. If your class were to make humus in a compost container, where would you put the humus?

Types of Roots

Get Started

Take a look at plants growing around you. You can see that they have different types of leaves. They are different colours, sizes, and shapes. Some plants grow flowers. Other plants grow nuts, fruit, or vegetables. You cannot see the roots of plants because they grow under the soil. Do you think the roots are different, too?

Work On It

Plant roots take in water and minerals from the soil. They hold the plant in place. The roots also help keep soil from blowing away in the wind or being washed away by water.

Some plants have roots that spread out under the surface of the soil to collect water. These are called **fibrous roots.**

Other plants have longer roots that are thick and grow deep in the soil. These are called **tap roots.**

Now you will look at the roots of two common plants.

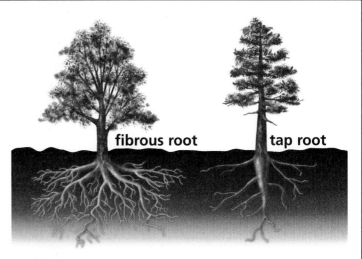

fibrous root   tap root

What You Need . . . .

- A trowel

What You Will Do . . . .

1 Use your trowel. Dig up a small patch of grass and a dandelion.

2 Look carefully at the roots of these plants. What do you see?

3 Draw a picture of the roots of the grass and the dandelion.

If you are doing this activity in winter, you can look at tap roots and fibrous roots by examining a carrot with the leaves still attached and a common indoor plant, such as a marigold.

Communicate

1. What kind of roots does the grass have?

2. What kind of roots does the dandelion have?

3. Label your drawings. Use the words *tap root* and *fibrous root*.

Who Lives in Soil?

Get Started

Soil is home to many different animals. Some live in the top of the soil. Others dig deep into the ground.

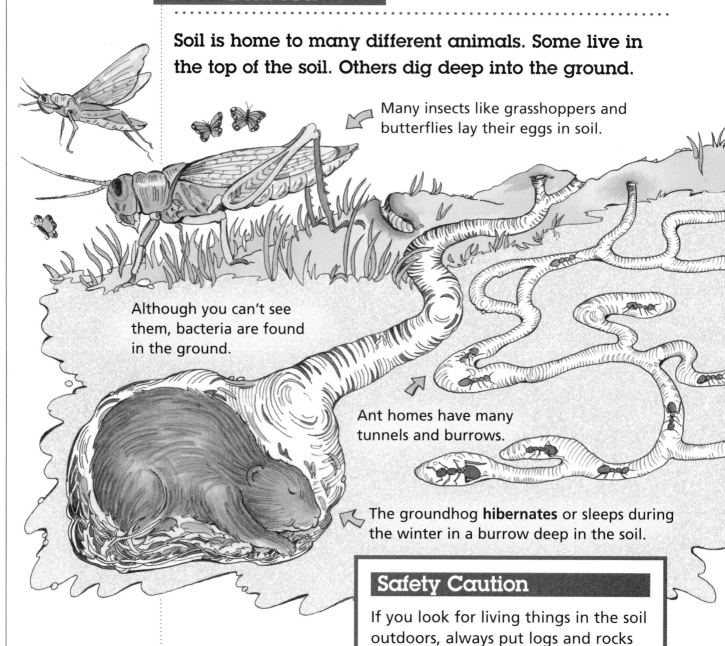

Many insects like grasshoppers and butterflies lay their eggs in soil.

Although you can't see them, bacteria are found in the ground.

Ant homes have many tunnels and burrows.

The groundhog **hibernates** or sleeps during the winter in a burrow deep in the soil.

Safety Caution

If you look for living things in the soil outdoors, always put logs and rocks quickly back where you found them.

Work On It

1. Look at the picture with a partner.

2. What living things can you find in the picture? Make a list.

Tiny creatures like mites and springtails live in the topsoil. They eat rotting plants and animals. This breaks them down into smaller pieces. Nutrients are added to the soil. Nutrients feed the plant so that it grows.

June bugs and dung beetles dig deep to make their nests and lay their eggs.

Badgers, moles, gophers, and rabbits also dig deep tunnels and burrows.

I live in soil, too!

Communicate

1. **a.** Can you think of other living things that are found in soil?

   b. Add them to your list.

2. **a.** Find rocks and logs outdoors. Lift them to look for living things.

   b. Draw pictures of what you find.

   c. Be sure to return rocks and logs to the place you found them.

Meet the Earthworms!

Get Started

Earthworms drag pieces of leaves and food into the soil. The leaves and pieces of food decay and make humus. Humus makes the soil richer with nutrients.

I've been waiting for this activity! Now you're going to meet my friends and family. Get ready to find out more about us.

You have learned about some creatures that live in the soil. The earthworm makes its home in the ground. Earthworms are important to gardens. Plants need air, water, and nutrients to grow. Earthworms help to provide these. On these pages, you will find out why.

Earthworms eat soil. As they eat the soil, they loosen it. This makes space for air and water to get into the soil. The soil earthworms do not use passes out of their bodies and returns to the soil. These droppings are good food for plants.

Earthworms need air to breathe. When it rains, air holes in the soil fill with water. This makes earthworms come up to the surface. Next time it rains, look out for earthworms!

You know earthworms are important because they mix nutrients, water, and air into the soil. In this investigation, you will watch to see how earthworms mix the soil.

What You Need

- A large clear jar
- Small rocks or pebbles
- Sand
- Soil
- Water
- Aluminum foil
- Tape
- Earthworms
- Worm food such as leaves

What You Will Do

1 How will you get earthworms? Work with your class to come up with ideas.

2 **a.** Put some small rocks or pebbles in the bottom of your jar.

b. Add sand and soil to make layers as shown in the picture here.

3 **a.** Add enough water to make the soil damp, but not too wet.

b. Put the worms in the jar and add some worm food.

4 Tape aluminum foil around the jar. Worms do not like the light.

5 **a.** Wait for one week. Take off the foil. How has the soil changed?

b. Draw a picture of what you see.

Earthworms need air and a moist skin. Add a few drops of water every day to the soil.

Communicate

1. Write about how the soil changed.

2. Why are earthworms good for soil?

3. Why do earthworms come to the surface of the soil after it rains?

11 Building with Earth Materials

Get Started

Look at these animal homes. They are partly made of mud. It makes sense, when you think about it. You can find mud almost everywhere. When mud dries, it becomes hard.

People also use earth materials to make shelters. Maybe humans got the idea from seeing animal homes.

This is an **adobe** home. Adobe is made of mud, grass, and straw. You can find adobe houses in warm places like the Southern United States or Africa.

This is a **brick** home. Bricks are made using **shale**, a hard clay. You will find brick buildings here in Canada.

People use earth materials to make useful things. Now it's your turn. You will use clay to make something useful.

What You Need

- Clay
- Water
- A plastic or wood board
- Tools for shaping and cutting clay

What You Will Do

1 Think about what you will make.

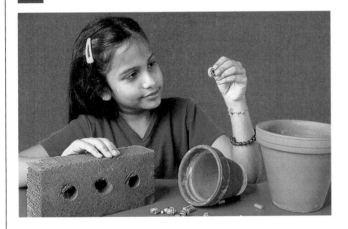

2 How will it be useful?

3 Draw a picture of what you would like your clay object to look like.

4 Make your object. Remember to keep the clay wet.

5 When you are finished, let the clay dry. You can paint it later. Your teacher might arrange to have your object fired in a kiln (a hot oven).

6 Check to see whether what you have made does what it is supposed to do.

Communicate

1. a. What problems did you have working with clay?

  b. How would you solve them next time?

2. a. Did the object you made do what it was supposed to do?

  b. If not, what would you do differently next time?

12 Erosion

Over time, moving water can cause many changes to rock. It can help pebbles form in rivers. It can break down rock so that sand forms on beaches.

Moving water in rivers transports soil and rocks to other places. It also rubs pebbles together. This makes them smooth.

Ocean waves beat on rocks and shells and slowly break them into tiny pieces. It takes millions of years to turn rocks and shells into sand. Ocean waves can also carry sand to different places.

Pebbles, sand, and soil take hundreds of years to form. But sometimes it doesn't take long for soil to be carried away. **Erosion** happens when soil moves. Moving water can cause erosion.

Too much rain can make soil and rocks slide down a slope. This is called a **landslide**.

Grass and other plants help to hold soil in place when it rains.

Floods happen when too much rain falls or snow melts. The soil cannot absorb the extra water.

Dykes are barriers that are built to prevent flooding. They can protect land from damage caused by moving water.

1. Look at the pictures on this page.

2. Discuss places that you know of that have been damaged by flooding or erosion.

Communicate

1. How does moving water affect earth materials?

2. How can people stop soil from being carried away by water?

Make a Soil Separator

Get Started

You have used water to separate soil into bits of sand, silt, and clay. Often, we use tools to separate things. You may have used these tools before.

What other types of sieves have you seen?

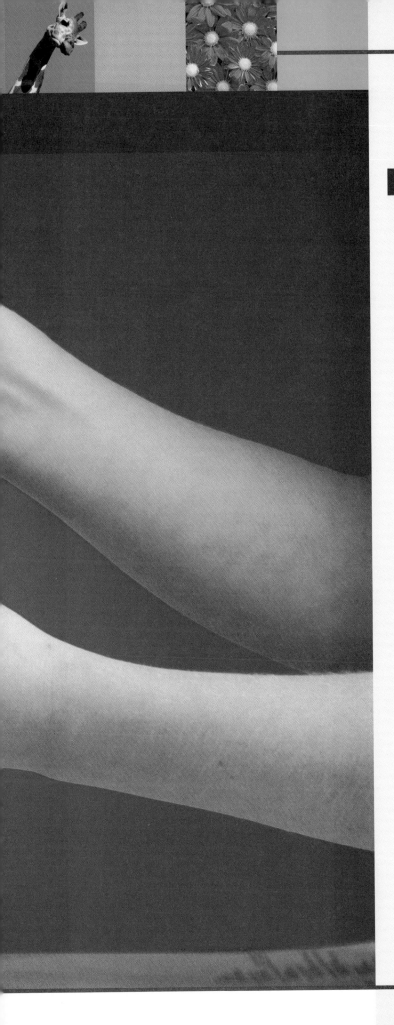

Work On It

Design It

Now you will have a chance to design and build a tool you can use to separate soil. You will make and use a tool called a sieve. Recording your ideas on paper will help you plan.

1. Look at Your Design Task below.

2. Look to see what your sieve must do. Record this information on your design sheet.

Your Design Task

Design and make a sieve that allows only the smallest bits of soil to pass through.

Your sieve must be able to:

- Hold a cup of soil to start
- Let only the smallest pieces of soil pass through

Design Project

Plan Your Design

1. Choose a container. Which one do you think will hold the soil well and will be easy to make good holes in?

2. Think about how you will make the holes. What size do you want them to be? You must also decide on the number of holes and where they should be.

3. Record your decisions.

Here are some of the things you might need to make your sieve. Are there other materials you would like to have?

Build Your Design

1. What problems did you have making your sieve?

2. Record your problems.

3. What did you do to solve them?

4. Record your solutions.

Safety Caution

Wear safety glasses to protect your eyes.

Make sure that the container is stable before you start making holes.

Be careful using sharp objects.

Always follow the safety rules your teacher tells you.

Test Your Design

1. Check to see that your sieve does what it is supposed to do. Do the right size pieces flow through it?

2. What changes would you like to make to your design?

3. Record whether your sieve works well.

Communicate

1. Demonstrate how your sieve works.

2. Think about the sieves your classmates made.
   a. How is your sieve like other sieves?
   b. Is your sieve unique in any way? If so, tell how it is different.

Design Project

How Well Did You Do?

Now it is time to see how well you did with your design project. Use this chart to help you score your work. Four stars is the highest score.

1 Star	2 Stars	3 Stars	4 Stars

SAFETY

1. a. How well did you follow the safety rules when you made your sieve?

You had to be reminded to follow the safety rules.	You followed some of the safety rules.	You followed most of the safety rules.	You followed all of the safety rules.

b. How safely did you use the hammer and nails?

You had to be reminded to use the equipment and the materials safely.	You used the equipment and the materials safely some of the time.	You used the equipment and the materials safely most of the time.	You used the equipment and the materials safely.

FINISHED SIEVE

2. How well does your sieve do what it is supposed to do?

I do not know what it is supposed to do.	It does none of the things it is supposed to do.	It does one of the things it is supposed to do.	It does both of the things it is supposed to do.

RECORDING YOUR DESIGN

3. a. Planning

You did not stop to make or record the planning decisions.

You made planning decisions but did not record them.

You made planning decisions but your recording is not complete.

You had a complete plan and recorded your decisions.

b. Building

You did not describe the challenges you had in building or how you solved them.

You described a challenge you had in building but not what you did to solve it.

You described a challenge you had during building and what you did to solve it.

You described two challenges you had during building and what you did to solve them.

c. Testing

You did not record how you tested your sieve.

You did not describe well how you tested your sieve.

You described well how you tested your sieve.

You described well how you tested your sieve. You also described how you would have changed it to make it even better.

Review

Demonstrate What You Know

Get Started

Here are some pictures showing some of the things you have learned in this unit.

Work On It

1. Look at the pictures on pages 34 and 35.

2. Write a sentence about each to show what you have learned about soil.

3. Be sure to include new words you have learned in your sentences.

Communicate

How well did you do? Use this information to score your work. Four stars is the highest score for each part.

Part 1

Give yourself four stars if you have written six facts about soil.

Part 2

Give yourself four stars if you have correctly used four new words in your sentences.

Part 3

Give yourself four stars if you have written three facts about how people use soil.

Review

Explain Your Stuff

What did you learn about soil?

1. What would you expect to find in a cup of soil from a garden near you?

2. Copy and complete these sentences:

   a. Sand is not very good for growing things because
   _____

   b. Clay is not good for growing things because
   _____

   c. Humus is made of
   _____

3. Finish this sentence:
   Soil contains _____, air, _____, and humus.

4. What do you think the soil is like in each of these places?

   a.

b.

c.

5. a. Draw a picture of the fibrous root of grass.

   b. Draw a picture of the tap root of a dandelion.

6. Write two reasons why you think your school should have a composter.

7. Name three creatures that live in the soil.

8. Write a sentence to describe how earthworms help gardeners.

How Did You Do?

1. List three things you didn't know about soil before this unit started.

2. Give one reason why what you learned about soil is important.

3. Which activity did you enjoy the most in this unit?

4. Write at least one question you would like answered about soil.

Now you know a lot about soil. Here are some of the things you've learned:

- Dead animals and plants decay and break down into tiny pieces to make humus.

- There are different kinds of soil.

- Soil can be separated into different parts.

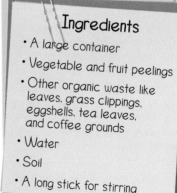

Ingredients
- A large container
- Vegetable and fruit peelings
- Other organic waste like leaves, grass clippings, eggshells, tea leaves, and coffee grounds
- Water
- Soil
- A long stick for stirring

- Adding compost to the soil helps make it even better for growing things.

- Roots of plants help to keep the soil in place.

- Earthworms help make soil richer.

- Soil is home to many different animals. Some live in the topsoil. Others dig deep into the soil.

- Too much rain can cause a landslide.

- People use soil to make many different things.

Glossary

adobe building material made from mud, grass, and straw used in warm countries

brick a building material made from shale

clay the component of soil that is sticky and is easily shaped when wet and that hardens after drying

composting the process of making humus from decaying plant matter to add to soil to make it richer

dyke barrier built to prevent flooding

fibrous root roots that are thread-like and that spread out in the soil

hibernate to spend the winter in sleep or in an inactive condition

humus the part of soil that consists of decayed organic material

landslide the sudden movement of soil and rocks down a slope because of rain

loam a type of soil used for gardening that contains a mixture of sand, clay, silt, and often humus

sand the component of soil that consists of gritty grains of worn-down rocks

shale a form of hard clay

silt the component of soil that consists of very fine, powdery earth or sand

tap root a very thick, deep root with tiny hairs that anchors the plant and can also store food

Acknowledgments

The publisher wishes to thank the following sources for photographs, illustrations, articles, and other materials used in this book. Care has been taken to determine and locate ownership of copyrighted material used in this text. We will gladly receive information enabling us to rectify any errors or omissions in credits.

Photography

p. 1 William J. Weber/Visuals Unlimited, p. 5 (top) Dave Starrett, p. 5 (centre and bottom) Ray Boudreau, p. 6 (top inset) Wendell Metzen/Bruce Coleman, p. 6 (top right) Glenn M. Oliver/Visuals Unlimited, p. 6 (bottom left) Publiphoto/Science Photo Library, p. 6 (bottom right) Linda Bailey/Animals Animals, p. 7 (top left) John Swedberg/Bruce Coleman, p. 7 (top right) Rolf Kopfle/Bruce Coleman, p. 7 (bottom) Breck P. Kent/Earth Scenes, p. 8 Dave Starrett, p. 9 Ray Boudreau, p. 10 (top left and right) Artbase Inc., p. 10 (bottom left) David Muench/CORBIS, p. 10 (bottom right) Andy Sacks/Tony Stone Images, p. 11 Ray Boudreau, p. 12 (left) Norman Owen Tomalin/Bruce Coleman, p. 12 (right) Laurie C. Dove/Garden Image, p. 14 B. Ivy/Ivy Images, p. 15 (top) Dave Starrett, p. 15 (centre) Ray Boudreau, p. 16 Dave Starrett, p. 18 (top from left to right) Lynn M. Stone/Bruce Coleman, Hans Reinhard/Bruce Coleman, Artbase Inc., Artbase Inc., p. 18 (bottom left to right) Artbase Inc., Artbase Inc., Eric Crichton/CORBIS, Douglas Peebles/CORBIS, p. 19 (inset) Gerald Tang/Garden Image, p. 19 (bottom) Artbase Inc., p. 22 Robert Pickett/CORBIS, p. 23 Ray Boudreau, p. 24 (top left) John Gerlach/Visuals Unlimited, p. 24 (top centre) John Shaw/Visuals Unlimited, p. 24 (top right) Steven Fuller/Animals Animals, p. 24 (bottom left) Robert Holmes/CORBIS, p. 24 (bottom right) Philippa Lewis; Edifice/CORBIS, p. 25 (top) Dave Starrett, p. 25 (centre and bottom) Ray Boudreau, p. 26 (top) Michael Gadomski/Earth Scenes, p. 26 (bottom) John Lemker/Earth Scenes, p. 27 (top left) Glenn M. Oliver/Visuals Unlimited, p. 27 (top right) Julie Eggers/Bruce Coleman, p. 27 (bottom left) Canadian Press CP, p. 27 (bottom right) Steve McCutcheon/Visuals Unlimited, pp. 28–29 Ray Boudreau, p. 30 Ray Boudreau, p. 31 Ray Boudreau, p. 34 (bottom left) Wendell Metzen/Bruce Coleman, p. 34 (bottom right) Robert Pickett/CORBIS, p. 35 (top) Julie Eggers/Bruce Coleman, p. 35 (centre) Robert Holmes/CORBIS, p. 35 (bottom) B. Ivy/Ivy Images, p. 36 (top) Breck P. Kent/Earth Scenes, p. 36 (centre) B. Ivy/Ivy Images, p. 36 (bottom) Rolf Kopfle/ Bruce Coleman, p. 37 (top left) Linda Bailey/Animals Animals, p. 37 (top right) Dave Starrett, p. 37 (bottom left) Ray Boudreau, p. 38 (centre left) Robert Pickett/CORBIS, p. 38 (bottom left) Glenn M. Oliver/Visuals Unlimited, p. 38 (bottom right) Ray Boudreau

Illustration

Tina Holdcroft: p. 1, pp. 2–3, p. 4, p. 8, p. 16, p. 17, pp. 20–21, p. 28, p. 34, p. 37, p. 38 (top right)
Cynthia Watada: p. 19, p. 38 (top left)

Cover Photograph

Gloria H. Chomica/Masterfile